Latest Liturgical Revision in the Church of England 1978-1984

by

Colin Buchanan

Principal, St. John's College, Bramcote, Notts.
Member of the Church of England Liturgical Commission

GROVE BOOKS

BRAMCOTE   NOTTS.   NG9 3DS

CONTENTS

INTRODUCTION

In 1973 I published Grove Booklet on Ministry and Worship no. 14, *Recent Liturgical Revision in the Church of England*. This was fatter than a usual booklet, and, having gone out of print, it is now being republished as a kind of Liturgical Study, with *'Down to 1973'* added to its title. After it, I produced three (standard-size) Booklets which were *'Supplements'* to Booklet 14—14A *(1973-4)*; 14B *(1974-6)*; and 14C *(1976-8)*. These three are still in print at normal Booklet price. Frequent reference to them is made in this Study. Somehow the opportunity never came to bring the story up to date, till a gap appeared in the Liturgical Study programme, and I have seized the chance. As before, no references are given to the General Synod *Report of Proceedings*, nor to my own monthly, *News of Liturgy*, both of which records can be easily perused. Also as before, I have been up to my neck in the middle of the events recorded—and only rarely as an impartial observer! In the past I acknowledged that I wrote 'not as a chronicler but as a journalist—though, I hope an accurate one . . .'. The acknowledgement and the hope are even more heartfelt here. I am in debt to many who have helped me, and I would be glad to know of errors in the account.

C.O.B.

First Impression September 1984

ISSN 0305-3067

ISBN 0 907536 75 1

1. THE PROGRAMME OF REVISION AS IT STOOD IN JULY 1978

This Liturgical Study consciously runs end-to-end with previous writings of mine, mentioned in the Introduction, which carried the story of the Church of England's official programme of revision down to the session of General Synod held in July 1978. Thus all that is here taken for granted, and the contents of this Study take up the story from that point. How then did the scene appear after the July 1978 session of General Synod?

The crucial governing factor in liturgical revision then was the timetable against which the Alternative Service Book was being prepared. Various Series 3 services were already authorized: Communion, Funerals, Morning and Evening Prayer, Collects, Marriage, and Ordination (from 1 September 1978). The Calendar and Lectionary had been authorized at that July 1978 session (from 28 October 1979).[1] Baptism and Confirmation were still in progress through in Synod.[2] Series 2 Communion had been revised by the Litugical Commission, and had just started its passage through Synod. And the timetable decreed that everything should reach 'Final Approval' in Synod in November 1979, in order that a full year for setting printing, binding, publishing, and distributing the ASB itself should elapse before the day then in view—1 November 1980. (This date itself ensured that the Synod of 1975-1980 which took the decision to have the Alternative Service Book would itself see the task to completion, and thus issues relating to the ASB and its services or its style of language could not enter the election of the new Synod in Spetember 1980.) Thus the following tasks had to be fulfilled:

(i) to complete the processes of authorization of Series 3 initiation services, and of Series 3 Revised communion.

(ii) to 'adapt' all Series 3 services, except communion, into conformity with the Series 3 Revised communion text.[3]

(iii) to tidy up the contents of the Book with a 'Miscellaneous Provisions' process.

(iv) to provide a 'Daily Eucharistic Lectionary'.[4]

(v) to agree on the question of a Psalter.[5]

(iv) to receive from the Liturgical Commission the choice of versions of the Bible for the various passages which were to be set out *in extenso* in the full ASB.

(vii) to provide a Preface, and to agree the order of contents and general arrangement.

1 See Booklets 14C pp.20-22. The only parts of this not authorized by July 1978 were (a) the Daily Eucharistic Lectionary (on which see chapter 4 below), and (b) the addition of opening and post-communion sentences to all the propers for holy communion (on which see chapter 3 below).

2 See Booklet 14C pp.14-17, and chapter 2 below. For fuller explanations see my Grove Booklet on Ministry and Worship 65, *Liturgy for Initiation: The Series 3 Services* (Grove Books, Bramcote, 1979).

3 See Booklet 14C pp.4-5, including the decision of Synod to allow 'adaptations' to be implemented by the 'shorter method'.

4 See footnote 1 above.

5 See Booklet 14C p.9 and chapter 4 below.

The first five of these tasks were for General Synod, the sixth for the Liturgical Commission, and the seventh for the Bishop of Durham's 'working group' which was responsible for the process of bring the ASB into action.[1]

Other tasks in liturgical revision were not directed towards the ASB. The most notable of these was provision for the liturgical needs of the sick and of those ministering to them. This task was to come to the Liturgical Commission in the years 1979-80, but with a view to the provision lying outside the actual ASB timetable and contents. The July 1978 Synod had also set in train another liturgical quest—for it responded to the 'Ten Propositions' on unity by passing on 10 July a composite motion which included the following:

'4 (b) That such recognition [i.e. of the ministers of the various Free Churches] will be effected by the action of the whole episcopate of all the covenanting Churches, incorporating (*cf.* GS 373 paragraphs 16 and 17) the existing ministers into the historic threefold ministry by invocation of the Spirit in a prayer which makes clear that such incorporation is intended and conveyed, by a distinctive sign for the conferring of a gift of the Spirit, and by concelebration of Holy Communion.'

It is with the way in which these tasks were handled that the rest of this Study is concerned.

---

[1] The 'Bishop of Durham' here and elsewhere in this Study was Dr. John Habgood, now Archbishop of York. The other members were: The Dean of York (Dr. Ronald Jasper), Messrs. H. S. Cranfield and R. Cross.

2. SERIES 3 INITIATION SERVICES

The early stages of this procedure are described in Booklet 14C. The report of the Revision Committee (GS 343X) and the revised text (GS 343A) were available for the July 1978 session of General Synod, but were crowded off the agenda then. So instead they came before Synod for the Revision Stage[1] on 7 and 10 November 1978. The main themes handled in the debate were:

  (i) the use of anointing permitted in opening Notes to baptism and to confirmation: Canon Peter Dawes had tabled an amendment to remove these provisions, but said that he 'deeply regretted' a public letter from the Catholic group in Synod to say that if his amendment were passed they would vote against the whole set of services. He bowed to such pressure and would not move his amendment.

  (ii) the protest by Professor Geoffrey Lampe against moving the signing with the cross to a position before the actual baptism, whilst allowing the use of oil, and in addition, explaining this change of position in the report as 'corresponding to the ancient position of exorcism'. It was 'exorcism' which raised his modern churchman's ire—he liked the placing of the signing with the sign of the cross there otherwise. He moved Peter Dawes' amendment but without success.

  (iii) The Bishop of Winchester moved the inclusion (among the prayers after the birth of stillborn child) of *'Prayers which may be used after the Medical Termination of a Pregnancy'*. He included a proposed text. He had already tried this on the Revision Committee, and been refused it.[2] It now came to full Synod, where it was also felt that such a prayer *as a matter of principle* seemed to connive at the principle of artificially induced abortion (which the Synod at other times opposed), and it was defeated on a count by Houses as follows:

	Ayes	Noes
Bishops	13	22
Clergy	71	109
Laity	90	75

  (iv) An attempt was made by the Rev. A. R. Heawood to remove the mention of the waters of the Red Sea from 'the blessing of the water', but this failed.

  (v) The Rev. Brian Brindley moved an amendment to the main interrogation which elicits the batismal affirmations of faith. The appositional nouns ('creator', 'redeemer') were thus changed to relative clauses ('who made the world', 'who redeemed mankind'). This was carried by 168 votes to 117.

1 For the details of the Synod's procedures in handling liturgy see Booklet 14A p.13, and its diagrammatic form in Booklet 14B p.16.

2 The actual text the Bishop proposed was:
  Heavenly Father,
  you are the giver of life
  and you share with us
  the care of the life that is given.
  Into your hands we commit in trust
  the developing life that we have cut short.
  Look in merciful judgment on the decision that we have made,
  and assure us in our uncertainty
  that your love for us can never change. Amen.

(vi) Finally, the Rev. R. E. Head attempted to move the central line of the confirmation prayer away from 'Let your Holy Spirit rest upon them'[1] and back to the Series 2 style 'Send down upon them your Holy Spirit'. At this point two anglo-catholic members, who in their own persons would have preferred the amendment, asked the Synod to bear in mind the unitive character of the text which was under attack in the amendment. Synod agreed and the amendment failed.

There were one or other tiny drafting amendments, but these were the main ones. The services then received 'Provisional Approval', and were remitted to the House of Bishops to be brought back for Final Approval at the next session. This occurred on 21 February 1979, when the services were authorized for a period from 3 June 1979 to 31 October 1980, by the following margins:

	Ayes	Noes
Bishops	29	0
Clergy	180	3
Laity	146	10

The booklet was advertised for publication on 17 May, and many places prepared for its use on 3 June (which was Pentecost Sunday). Sadly, the services were not published till 21 June. They came out in a booklet published by the Privileged Presses and by S.P.C.K. called *Initiation Services: Alternative Services Series 3* (AS 330). This was the first use of ASB format, with a slightly deeper page than the previous Series 3 services had exhibited. It was followed up with offprints of the infant baptism rite (AS 331, on a card) and the 'confirmation only' rite (AS 341, a short booklet).

When the services came to be 'adapted' for inclusion in the ASB, then the following most obvious changes were made[2]:
  (i) *Thanksgiving Serivces* (ASB pages 212-222):
    (a) An opening 'Note'[3] about the version of the Lord's Prayer is now covered on page 32.
    (b) The rubric at no. 3 about a choice of items has been changed, and what were nos. 3, 4, and 5 are now simply no. 3, affecting all section numbers thereafter.
    (c) The text of the Lord's Prayer has been changed.[4]
    (d) The suggested readings (nos. 15 and 29 in ASB) are listed after each service, instead of only after the second.

[1] This had been deliberately drawn from the Isaiah 11 background to avoid what were thought to be the obvious pitfalls of 'Send down . . .' *and* of 'Strengthen them with . . .'.

[2] The adaptations were contained in GS 393, published in December 1978, given general consideration, revision in full Synod, and and provisional approval on 23 February 1979. Final Approval came on 5 July 1979 by: Bishops 22-0; Clergy 112-2; Laity 140-3.

[3] In other words, once several services were being published together between one set of covers, there were many common rubrics which could be printed once for the whole book, and this affected all the services, and is mentioned on p.14 below.

[4] This is described on pp.11-12 below, and the 'adaptation' was in accord with the overall policy expounded in chapter 1 above.

(ii) *The Prayers after the Birth of a Stillborn Child* (ASB pages 322-323) are now to be found after The Funeral of a Child.

(iii) *The Main Initiation Services* (ASB pages 225-235):

    (a) Opening Note 9 (about the significance of numbers printed in blue) is now on ASB page 32.[1]

    (b) The section numbering changes at 16, where the rubric was included under 15 in AS330, and at 41, where it was included under 39.

    (c) In 'The Communion' cross-references are now to Rite A and Rite B, not to Series 3.[2]

(iv) *The Baptism of Children* (ASB pages 241-251):

    (a) The special provisions of pages 250 and 251 were in AS 330 printed before the rite, not after it. But the propers for communion were printed after it.

    (b) Some of the psalms and readings (ASB pages 261-274) were grouped with the propers to follow the infant baptism rite.

(v) *Confirmations* (ASB pages 250-260):

    (a) The propers (including the other readings now in ASB on pages 261-274) follow the rubric for the blessing and dismissal.

The unamended Series 3 services on 7 November 1979 had their period extended to 'the date of publication the of the Alternative Service Book'.[3] The adapted text went into the list of contents of the ASB, which were authorized together from the date of publication to 31 December 1990.[4]

---

[1] See footnote 3 on page 6 above.

[2] The addition of 'Rite B' here might be viewed as a somewhat cavalier 'adaptation'. It is impossible now to imagine who had the bright idea that some bishop might want to combine a modern confirmation with an ancient eucharist. It is unlikely it has ever happened. But the ASB is clearly ready for *all* eventualities.

[3] See page 23 below.

[4] See page 21 below.

3. FROM SERIES 3 COMMUNION TO RITE A

The revision of Series 3 was planned as the centre-piece of the whole preparation for the ASB.[1] It was intended throughout the revision of it that the resultant text, when authorized, should be the text within the ASB to which all other rites in modern language were then confomred by 'adaptation'. Thus a single standard presentation of all rites, including Notes, rubrics, and text of recurrent items, like the Lord's Prayer, would be relatively easily achieved. Equally, the timetable was due to be under pressure, as the text of this rite had, in principle, to be agreed *before* other 'adaptations' could take place, and thus the rite would not be allowed to drag out its synodical processes to the last minute.

The early stages of the revision—from Autumn 1976 to July 1978—are described in 14C.[2] The changes made from Series 3 to the report of the Commission (GS 364) were in fact relatively modest, and they modelled that which was often breathed around, that what Synod was attempting was a 'light revision'. But the prescient could well envisage that, once 550 members of General Synod each had the chance to suggest amendments, the combined effect of the 'light' changes wanted by each of them might yet prove to be very heavy indeed. And, indeed, a 'light revision' never was, and never could have been, official policy—at most it was a 'fond' notion of Standing Committee. The standing orders gave every scope to members to flex all their muscles for revising purposes, and without either *definition* of 'light', or procedures to restrict the process of revision, it was certain that it would be more than 'light'.

After the debate on 11 July 1978 the text of GS 364 was accorded 'General Consideration' and was remitted to its 'Revision Committee', chaired by the Bishop of Derby.[3] Within the Revision Committee, the 'Steering Committee' consisted of four members, chaired by me.[4] Later, the Bishop of Derby was also added to the Steering Committee. When the required 35 days were up, somewhere between 1000 and 1200 amendments desired by members of Synod had been received at Church House. The Revision Committee duly started its meetings in September, but it quickly became

---

[1] See Booklet 14C, p.4, and chapter 1 above.

[2] Booklet 14C includes some of the behind-the-scenes history, and there is also a brief description in my Booklet 68, *Liturgy for Communion: The Revised Series 3 Service* (Grove Books, Bramcote, 1979).

[3] For the procedures see Booklet 14A, p.12. However, it should be noted that relatively few amendments (by later standards) were received for services up to and including the ordination services (for which the Revision Committee completed its work virtually within a calendar month). But then Synod started to flex its muscles and discover its strength! For the initiation services somewhere around 300 amendments were received (in November and December 1977). Meanwhile the Calendar and Lectionary material had received even more (see Booklet 14C p.20) and it took a *year* to report. And thus everyone knew that these excesses were but a light overture to what was to be expected when the eucharistic revision started . . .

[4] The chairman of the Steering Committee introduces the text to Synod at 'General Consideration', then works to enable the Revision Committee to do its work. When the Revision Stage is reached he or she 'steers' the Revision Committee's text through Synod.

clear that the sheer difficulty of receiving and hearing all would-be movers of amendments, let alone of debating and voting on their amendments—let alone again doing the detailed consequential drafting of other amendments to keep consistency of presentation and wording—would almost certainly bog down the Committee and prevent it from reporting (as it almost certainly *had* to do) to the February 1979 session of Synod.[1] Thus the Steering Committee devised an alternative and corner-cutting procedure: we usually drafted out own 'mainstream' text *in advance of Committee meetings,* got it accepted as 'on the table', indicated all the variety of proposed amendments that would thus be swallowed up and fall, and, in effect, dared anyone (Committee member or synodsman) to try then to amend *our* text: sometimes instead we produced texts in parallel columns, and worked our way in full Committee through the choices thus given to the members.

One notable event attained some public discussion during the period of the Committee's work. In November 1978, there was released to the press (at the same time as being presented to the Committee) a 'deal' between the Rev. Brian Brindley, a member of the Committee and a noted and colourful anglo-catholic, and the Rev. Roger Beckwith, warden of Latimer House Oxford, not a member of Synod, a well-known evangelical who had consistently opposed Series 3 communion as unbiblical. The thrust of the 'deal' was this:

(a) Brian Brindley would promote in the Revision Committee a 'modernized 1662' text—this would help those of Roger Beckwith's persuasion, and in particular deliver 1662-lovers from the appearance of being immovable on questions of *language,* when in fact a proportion of them wanted modern language services, but *not* an alteration of the doctrine or contents or structure of the 1662 rite.

(b) Roger Beckwith in return would assent to Brian Brindley's simultaneous promotion of a new eucharistic prayer (by Roman Catholic Eucharistic Prayer II out of Hippolytus), which would not be to his own taste, but would be sufficiently doctored for him to agree that its use would not be inimical to the doctrinal position of the Church of England.

The 'deal' was an asymmetrical one, as the Revision Committee had *already agreed to part (a) of it,* and thus only (b) was new. But presumably the pair of authors agreed with each other that they were acting in symmetry. The Revision Committee, for its part, whilst noting that the House of Bishops had earlier rejected a whole range of other eucharistic prayers[2], and whilst refusing itself to accept any other ones not in GS 364 (bar a slightly shortened one for use with the sick), yet allowed Brian Brindley to promote this Hippolytan text, and, after some revision, added it to the

---

1 This was imperative in order to get Final Approval by July 1979, in order that other texts could be 'adapted' from it. There was *just* room for the Revision Stage to spill over from February to July (as it ultimately did), which would bring the Final Approval to November 1979, but to delay beginning the Revision Stage to July 1979 would give no elbow-room for adjourning the debate at all.

2 See Booklet 14C, p.13.

rite.[1] The modernized forms of the eucharistic prayers from Series 1 (with the two endings turned into one without self-oblation)and from Series 2 were also brought into the main text, thus providing the rite with four eucharistic prayers.

Another feature of the work of the Revision Committee was the provision of opening and post-communion sentences of scripture for all occasions for which readings and a collect were authorized.

There were other tricky doctrinal questions to resolve. The one which has loomed largest has always been the text of the anamnesis paragraph—and now there were *four* to agree. However, it was concerning the text of the first eucharistic prayer that the greatest concern was registered. It was also, of course, the point at which the House of Bishops had affected the drafting prior to the publication of the Liturgical Commission's report, GS 364.[2] This in turn meant that the members of the Steering Committee (which included three members of the Liturgical Commission out of the total of four) knew how to recapture the original agreements achieved on the Liturgical Commission, and agreement was duly achieved again. There were evangelical concerns about the wording of the Hippolytan prayer, and the problem here was over the words of Roman provenance 'We bring before you this bread and this cup'. However, evangelicals contented themselves with getting the invocation of the Spirit upon the elements (which Roger Beckwith had underwritten originally) changed into an invocation upon the recipients. And there remained the problem of the 'offertory'.[3] On the Revision Committee many wanted the Roman 'offertory prayers'[4], whilst many others wanted no directions or words beyond the bare statement that the elements were to be made ready on the Holy Table. A cross-current still blew the text of Chron. 29.11, 14 across

[1] For the text as originally proposed by Beckwith and Brindley see Liturgical Study no. 20 *The Development of the New Eucharistic Prayers of the Church of England* (Grove Books, Bramcote, 1979).

[2] See Booklet 14C, p.13.

[3] GS 364 had the word 'offertory' inserted into its rubrics at the insistence of the House of Bishops (who had earlier insisted on it in 'Series 1 and Series 2 Revised'). The word was acknowledged on all sides to be ambiguous, and was duly eliminated again. When the word is understood to mean some kind of 'offering up' to God of the unconsecrated bread and wine it is also controversial (see my Liturgical Study no. 14, *The End of the Offertory* (Grove Books, Bramcote, 1978)—drafted and published in exactly the weeks between the publication of GS 364 and the first debating of it in Synod.

[4] The Roman Catholic texts described are:

(for the bread) Blessed are you, Lord, God of all creation
Through your goodness we have this bread to offer,
which earth has given and human hands have made.
It will become for us the bread of life.
Blessed be God for ever.

(for the cup) Blessed are you, Lord, God of all creation.
Through your goodness we have this wine to offer,
fruit of the vine and work of human hands.
It will become our spiritual drink.
Blessed be God for ever

the Committee's path, but that deflecting force was easily resisted.[1] The main point was met by the wholly unprincipled expedient of printing the *response* to the Roman Prayers (i.e. 'Blessed be God for ever') without having first printed four lines of versicle in each case! Thus the lovers of the Roman words got a strong hint that there was only one verbal route by which they could reach the response, whilst the loathers of the versicle were not being asked to agree to its inclusion.[2]

Many other features of the rite were tightened in their rubrical provision, or loosened by the use of 'Notes' making variants non-penal, and an ever-growing appendix of alternate uses started to rival the main text in length. The 'modernized 1662' was duly slotted into the rite with its own text set out in full, and not just by rubric, and it was embellished by the use of the word *'priest'* in the rubrics.[3] Finally, the Committee managed to present an opening sentence and a post-communion sentence for every occasion for which a collect and readings was being authorized.[4]

The revised text, GS 364A, (with the expanded propers in GS 364B), accompanied by an understandably lengthy report justifying all the re-drafting (GS 364X), was published on 8 February 1979, ready for the February session of General Synod.

The Revision Stage in General Synod came on 21 and 22 February, and around 200 amendments were sent in before the day, and the Steering Committee prepared fall-back positions with their own platform amendments tabled. The Bishop of Derby introduced the report of the Revision Committee, and then, between the February and July sessions, nineteen hours were used in full Synod to go through the Revision Stage. The most notable alterations were those which shifted four lines from the First Eucharistic Prayer to the second.[5] and amended the ninth line of the Lord's Prayer from the ICET text ('Save us from the time of trial') to the

---

1 In other words, the 1 Chron. 29 passage (about gifts not of symbolic but of *substantial* value) which in Series 3 had been attached to the bread and wine (incorrectly in my opinion) was now provided solely in relation to the collection of money.

2 . . . and the Steering Committee was equipped to resist amendments which either sought to include the Roman prayers, or sought to delete the whole odd provision.

3 There was an element of irony behind this. Some anglo-catholics had alleged that the departure (in Series 3) from the Prayer Book word *'priest'* in favour of *'president'* was a departure from a doctrinal norm, and possibly implied a covert whittling away at the supposed doctrine of priesthood. The Committee gave them what they wanted, in precisely the place where their argument led—that is, the 1662 material kept the *'priest'* rubrical form. The irony lies in that the persons concerned are of all Anglicans those least likely to favour the use of the modernized 1662.

4 Two members divided the task. He who got Advent to Pentecost drew heavily on the Roman Missal. He who got the Pentecost season (with Sunday themes unrelated to the Missal—to which he might well not have gone anyway)—drew upon his own wit, making his own translations of the Greek of the New Testament as he went along. Hence these sentences do not exhibit a single (or even multiple) version of the Bible as their source. See page 18 below.

5 The exact changes from one stage to the next can be seen in my *The Development of the New Eucharistic Prayers of the Church of England* (Grove Liturgical Study 20, 1979).

more traditionalist 'Lead us not into temptation'.[1] There was considerable defensive work to be done, not least in resisting efforts on both sides to clarify the section which concealed the Roman offertory prayers[2], in seeing off a somewhat tendentious 'Eucharistic Prayer to be used with Children', and in deflecting the thin end of a wedge which threatened to insert the slippery concept of 'concelebration' into the opening notes.[3]

The Ju:y session of Synod included this Revision procedure on 2, 4, 5, and 6, July 1979, and concluded it with a vote for 'Provisional Approval'. On a show of hands only one hand amongst around 300 was seen in dissent. The House of Bishops made fourteen tiny drafting amendments and brought the service before Synod in November 1979 for Final Approval. The vote on 7 November 1979 was to authorize the rite from 1 May 1980 to 'the date of the publication of the Alternative Service Book'. Voting was: Bishops 33-4; Clergy 207-10; Laity 150-23. Then on 9 November the rite was included in the pantechnicon vote which gave currency to all ASB services from the date of publication of ASB to 31 December 1990, which is the theme of the next two chapters.[4]

Rite A, as the revised Series 3 was now entitled, was published in booklet form and came into use on 1 May 1980, in accordance with the first of the General Synod decisions recorded above. The booklet was a kind of 'pre-offprint' of the ASB, appearing before the full Book, but in every respect reflecting it—beginning the text of the service on page 119, and using the page size and format of the Book. The 'General Rubrics' of the ASB were reproduced before the service itself began.[5] The booklet was coded 'ASB 20'. The first edition had various errors in the text, though these have been largely corrected since.[6]

---

[1] This text represented a step backwards from both the Series 3 line, 'Do not bring us to the time of trial', and the ICET version. However, it was arguably an improvement on the Commission's 'Let us not be led into temptation' (which was in GS 364). Whilst it is not the best translation, yet it was the best modern version that offered hope of getting the lovers of the ancient to accept the modern. In other words it was the best text *on which the Synod could agree.* Comically enough, no member of Synod had sent it in as an amendment and the chairman of the Steering Committee (see page 8) had tabled it as a 'fall-back' lest the Synod maroon itself in a backwater. A strong attempt to print a traditional text of the Lord's Prayer alongside it was defeated.

[2] See page 10 above.

[3] See pages 36-37 below.

[4] See page 21 below.

[5] See page 14 below.

[6] See footnote 3 on page 22 below.

4. PUTTING TOGETHER
THE ALTERNATIVE SERVICE BOOK

The working group under the Bishop of Durham had to decide, between Februvry 1976 and November 1979, the exact contents and lay-out of the Alternative Service Book, and to devise a synodical (as well as a publishing and publicizing) procedure for getting it all into shape and into print and into use aright. This can be set out here best by taking the contents of the final book, and annotating each part in order.

(a) The Preface (pages 9-11)
This came last, was never 'authorized' (as it is not a service!), and has been generally attributed to the chairman of the working group. The Liturgical Commission commented on earlier drafts. An interesting point on page 10 is the claim that the Book gives considerable evidence as to the 'mind of the Church of England in the last quarter of the twentieth century'.

(b) The Calendar and Rules to Order the Services (page 13-29) and Lectionaries (pages 979-1093)
This material was produced between 1976 and 1978, and was originally authorized in July 1978 from 28 October 1979 to 31 October 1980.[1] It was not then published as a separate document, but, of course, controlled the annual *Almanack* and diary entries. In order to give the ASB a flying start in 1980, the 1979 start was for 'Year Two'. Then on 7 November 1979 the period was extended to 31 October 1982.[2] Meanwhile the process of 'adaptation' led to tiny amendments and Provisional Approval on 23 February 1979 and to Final Approval on 5 July 1979.[3] The adapted form then joined the contents of the ASB which gained Provisional Approval on 8 November 1979 and Final Approval on 9 November 1979 for authorization from the 'date of the publication of the' ASB until 31 December 1990.[4]

There was an element in the Calendar, the Rules to Order the Service, and Lectionary, which did not follow the above path exactly. This was the 'Daily Eucharistic Lectionary'. The decision in principle to include the Roman Catholic daily provision was made on 3 February 1978, and the report from the Liturgical Commission, which attempted to fit the Roman Catholic material into the new ASB 'Alternative Calendar' (but in such a way that the Roman Catholic readings would be used on the same day as they would in the Church of Rome), was given General

---

1 See Booklet 14C, pp.21-22. The October start reflected the 'ninth Sunday before Christmas'—the end reflected the expectation that the ASB would come into force on 1 November 1980.

2 Bishops 30-0; Clergy 117-0; Laity 117-1. The extended date gave a breathing space if the ASB were not to come into existence, and gave ample room (on the assumption it would exist) for it to be published later than 1 November 1980 (see footnote 1 above). The period was to assist publishers of diaries.

3 Bishops 22-0; Clergy 112-2; Laity 140-3.

4 The voting on this is recorded on page 21 below.

Consideration on 23 February 1979. It was revised in full Synod on 2 July 1979 and then given Provisional Approval. Final Approval (for a period from 1 December 1979 to 31 October 1982) came on 5 November 1979.[1] Then it joined the other materials for inclusion in the ASB.[2]

(c) General Notes (pages 31-33)

The General Notes are in part taken from the Notes of particular Series 3 services.[3] Some however are not instructions concerning services, but relate to the interpretation of the ASB's conventions. No. 10 is drawn from the original introduction to the Collins' *The Psalms: A New Translation for Worship.*

(d) Sentences (pages 35-43)

The seasonal sentences have been collected together from Series 3 Morning and Evening Prayer and Series 3 Holy Communion. In the case of Communion, the sentences here (in which Series 3 were printed in the rite) represent uses for high seasons. Whilst the eucharistic rite was being revised by the Revision Committee[4], a proposal was accepted to provide introductory and post-communion sentences for every occasion which had Propers at all. Thus the seasonal sentences lost their place in the rite itself, and were, by editorial action, moved to the present place in the ASB.

(e) Morning and Evening Prayer (pages 45-95)

Series 3 Morning and Evening Prayer were originally authorized from 1 November 1975 to 31 December 1979, and were published in a yellow booklet.[5] They were in a list of 'Existing Authorized Services' which had their authorization extended on 7 November 1979 to 'the date of the publication of the Alternative Service Book'.[6] Meanwhile the 'adaptation' procedure had begun on 11 July 1978.[7] These adaptations received Final Approval on 21 February 1979.[8] The effects were minimal, though the change in the Lord's Prayer and the confession, to conform them to the style of Rite A, were the most notable. The addition of 1662 canticles (pages 88-95) was for convenience.

(f) Prayers for Various Occasions (pages 97-107)

A further set of 'adaptations' under this title produced the collection of prayers. The report (GS 393) was published in December 1978 and was

---

[1] The period corresponds to that for the rest of the Calendar and Lectionary material at this stage (see footnote 2 on page 13 above). The voting was: Bishops 27-0; Clergy 138-2; Laity 136-0.

[2] See page 21 below.

[3] As, for instance, six are drawn from Morning and Evening Prayer, where the 'adaptation' ran as follows 'Notes, 1, 2, 4, 13, 14, 16 to be removed and form part of *General Notes* for the whole book' (GS 362, page 7). For the process with respect to these services see paragraph (e) following next but one after this present one. (These six became nos. 3, 2, 1 (in part), 9, 5, and 16 (in part), in the ASB respectively).

[4] See chapter 3 above.

[5] See Booklet 14B, p.10.

[6] This imprecise date was chosen to secure the situation if something went wrong with the publication schedule. See chapter 5 below.

[7] See Booklet 14C, page 8., re GS 362.

[8] The voting was: Bishops 32-0; Clergy 172-3; Laity 149-5.

generally considered, then revised in full synod, and provisionally approved, on 23 February 1979. Final approval came on 5 July 1979.[1] The general effect was to take the litany out of Morning and Evening Prayer, and add other useful prayers. A further report, *Alternative Service Book: Miscellaneous Provisions* (GS 405), added some material not in the existing services.[2] This report was generally considered on 6 July 1979. It was revised in full Synod, and provisionally approved on 7 November 1979. Final approval came on 9 November 1979.[3] Its contents then became part of the services included in the ASB.

(g) Subject Index for Prayers (pages 109-112)

This wes an original part of GS 405, just mentioned. Like the table of contents, an index can only be completed during the production process (in order to get page numbers right), and this was the responsibility of the working group.

(h) The Order for Holy Communion Rite A (pages 113-173)

The stages of preparation of this rite are described in chapter 3 above. The last stage of authorization in November 1979 are described on page 21 below. The separate booklets of Rite A (coded ASB 20, and with page numbering showing it to be an 'offprint' from the rite in the ASB itself[4]) were published on 1 May 1980, six months before the actual Book. The text included some errors at that stage, but they have been reduced in the successive editions of the ASB itself.

(i) The Order for Holy Communion Rite B (pages 175-210)

The original proposed table of contents of the ASB in February 1976 included 'Holy Communion Series 1 and 2 Revised'.[5] At that point the rite had received provisional approval only two days before, and had yet to gain final approval. In the event, this was only secured in July 1976 by a decimal point of a clergyman.[6] So the rite embarked on a life of being a survivor. The booklets were published on 21 October 1976, and the rite was authorized from 1 November 1976 to 31 December 1979. The relevant adaptations were published in August 1978 in GS 380. At many points the thrust of these was to conform notes and rubrics to the ultimate outcome of the process leading to Rite A. Parallel columns, such as the booklet possessed, were to be abolished. Proper Prefaces were to be removed to an appendix.[7] On the other hand, certain matters could not be guessed easily in Summer 1978, a time preceding the work of the Revision Committee on Rite A. Thus no opening position for penitence was provided, no permission to use any suitable forms of intercession was provided, and no invitation to exchange the Peace followed the usual text. The

---

1 The voting was: Bishops 22-0; Clergy 112-2; Laity 140-3.
2 The report contained various additions to several services, and acquired more whilst being revised in Synod. It was affectionately known on the Liturgical Commission as the 'rat-bag'.
3 The voting was: Bishops 11-0; Clergy 103-1; Laity 110-4.
4 'Offprint' is in inverted commas because the full Book did not exist at the time.
5 See Booklet 14B, p.12.
6 The requisite two-thirds majority was achieved in the House of Clergy by 105-52!
7 They were still called 'Proper Thanksgivings' in the rules on page 28 of the ASB.

ambiguous word 'Offertory' still came in association with putting the bread and wine on the holy table, the title 'Eucharistic Prayer' did not supersede 'The Thanksgiving', and the appendices are thinner than those of Rite A. Some of these points became a minor problem in the 1980s.[1] The adaptions came before Synod for general consideration, revision in full synod, and provisional approval, on 23 February 1979. Final approval came in the morning of 4 July 1979.[2] However, in the afternoon of the same day, the Synod was asked by the Bishop of Durham to debate a general motion on the ASB, and I moved an amendment to delete Rite B from the contents of the Book.[3] There had been some disquiet about its role as the only 'thou' form text in the Book for some time.[4] And its earlier bare survival at final approval also gave cause for pause.[5] The amendment was defeated by 162 votes to 127.[6]

The unamended '1 and 2 Revised' was in the list of 'existing authorized services' which on 7 November 1979 had their licence extended from 31 December 1979 to 'the date of the publication of the Alternative Service Book'.[7] The adapted text, now to be known as Rite B, joined the list of services for inclusion in the Book which were authorized together from the date of publication to 31 December 1990.[8]

(j) Initiation Services (pages 211-281)

These are described in chapter 2 above, including the detail of their adaptation for inclusion in the ASB. The adaptations were included in GS 393, published in December 1978, before the unadapted services had yet received final approval in Synod. GS 393 came before Synod for general consideration, revision in full synod, and provisional approval, on 23 February 1979, and went on to final approval on 5 July 1979.[9] The unadapted text had its period extended on 7 November 1979 to the date of the publication of the ASB (adding ten days to its life in this particular case).[10] And the adapted texts went into the list of contents of the ASB which were authorized together from the date of publication to 31 December 1990.[11]

[1] The extent of the adaptations can be seen at a glance in the text of Rite B published in my forthcoming *Latest Anglican Liturgies* 1975-1984 (Alcuin/SPCK), where '1 and 2 Revised' is shown as an *apparatus* to Rite B.

[2] The voting was: Bishops 33-0; Clergy 164-1; Laity 156-3.

[3] It was acknowledged that this was the first chance the Synod had had to rule on its inclusion since the rite had first been authorized, and my argument was that its inclusion was a cosmetic gesture rather than a useful addition to the contents.

[4] See Booklet 14C, p.6, footnote 2.

[5] See footnote 6 on page 15 above.

[6] This vote might have encouraged me to one more synodical move. As it was less than a two-thirds majority, it might have been appropriate to have asked that in November 1979, when the list of contents of the Book came up for a single vote to authorize them to 1990, this particular service should have been subject to a separate vote, lest it did not in fact have a two-thirds majority in particular Houses for its inclusion. It could still have been authroized as a separate booklet for a shorter period. I think the request would have been reasonable and should have been granted! But I did not make it.

[7] See the process described on page 23 below.

[8] See the process described on page 21 nelow.

[9] See under Calendar and Lectionary on page 13 above.

[10] See the process described on page 23 below.

[11] See the process described on page 21 below.

(k) The Marriage Service (pages 283-304)

The Series 3 Marriage service was authorized in 1977 for use from 1 November 1977 to 31 December 1979, and was published as a blue booklet on 13 October 1977.[1] Its adaptations were contained in GS 380, the progress of which is described above under the Rite B heading. Their effect was minimal. The unadapted service had its period extended on 7 November 1979 to the date of the publication of the ASB, and the adapted text went into the list of contents of the ASB which were authorized together from the date of publication to 31 December 1990.[2]

(l) Funeral Services (pages 305-336)

The original Series 3 Funeral services were authorized in 1975, and their period was extended in 1976 to 31 December 1979.[3] Their adaptations came in GS 362 and followed the same course as those for Morning and Evening Prayer described above. The effects were minimal, though the adaptation of Series 3 Initiation services and the *Miscellaneous Liturgical Proposals*[4] brought 'Prayers after the Birth of a still-born Child or the Death of a newly-born Child' into the set of Funeral services.[5] The unadapted text had its period extended on 8 November 1979 to the date of the publication of the ASB, and the adapted text went into the list of contents of the ASB which were authorized together from the date of publication of the ASB.[6]

(m) The Ordinal (pages 337-396)

The Series 3 Ordination services received final approval in July 1978, and were authorized from 1 September 1978 to 31 December 1979.[7] They were never published in booklet form.[8] Their adaptations were printed in GS 380, the course of which is described above under Rite B. The effect of them was almost invisible. The unadapted text was extended on 7 November 1979 to the date of the publication of the ASB, and the adapted text went into the list of contents of the ASB which were authorized together from the date of publication of the ASB.[9]

(n) Sentences, Collects, and Readings (pages 397-978)

There are nearly 600 pages of these Propers, virtually half the Book. The 1976 resolution that the Book should appear in two versions—one with, one without, such readings *in extenso*—got lost on the way to authorization and production, and all versions include these 600 pages.[10] The materials came to be placed here by differing routes.

---

1 See Booklet 14C, p.18.

2 See the processes described on pages 23 and 21 below respectively.

3 See Booklets 14B, p.10, and 14C, p.22.

4 See page 15 above.

5 This was the original intention—see Booklet 14C, p.17.

6 See the processes described on pages 23 and 21 below respectively.

7 See Booklet 14C, p.19.

8 Not only so, but all reproduction of them was *forbidden.* I attempted to put the text into Booklet 60 *Liturgy for Ordination,* but was refused permission (see Booklet 60, p.2).

9 See the processes described on pages 23 and 22 below respectively.

10 This was reported in GS 413 in May 1979—see page 23 below. It is strongly arguable that a Book half the thickness would have met many needs very well, not least those of congregations with pew Bibles with standard pagination, and that Synod was deprived of something which had been clearly in view in both the researches of the working party before 1976 and in the February 1976 debate.

The Sentences were produced by the Revision Committee on Rite A, and formed a separate document (GS 364B) which was revised in Synod near the end of the Rite A Revision Stage, on 5 and 6 July 1979. They were thus authorized with Rite A, and it is an open question whether strictly speaking they have any status in relation to Rite B.[1] They come from many versions of scripture, and sometimes from none![2]

The Collects were originally published as a separate booklet in January 1977, being authorized from 1 February 1977 to 31 December 1979. Additional collects were needed when the Alternative Calendar and Lectionary were provided, and these were published in GS 405, *Miscellaneous Liturgical Proposals,* and authorized in the way described under 'Prayers for Various Occasions' above.

The Readings were all authorized under the Lectionary provisions described above. The Liturgical Commission worked on the various passages to determine which versions of scripture would read aloud best.[3] They employed a considerable proportion of NEB readings, which history may yet deem to have been a mistake. No reading was to be used which at any point addressed God as 'thou', though the RSV copyright holders were willing for 'thou' to be changed to 'you' in extracts from their version. Clearly, there is no necessity to use the versions printed, and congregations are at liberty to use any permitted version.[4]

(o) Tables (pages 979-1093)

In general these set out the lectionary provision already covered in this description.[5] Table 5 (pages 1092-1093) more strictly belongs with the collects and readings, but a decision of the Revision Committee on the Calendar and Lectionary in 1978 separated the list of themes from the actual propers.[6] Thus the table is now coyly tucked into the very back of the Book. Preachers are not supposed to be distracted by the theme title over a passage of scripture when they are wrestling with it, but after they have done their work they can look up the answers at the back of the Book and see if they got the solution right . . .

(p) The Liturgical Psalter (pages 1095-1289)

This Psalter was in the 1976 list of contents, before it was published as a

---

[1] In Rite B, rubric 43 has specific cross-reference to 'pp.42, 43', i.e. to the block collection of Sentences (mentioned on page 14 above), whereas in Rite A rubric 50 has no such reference, and presumably refers in the first instance to the serried propers.

[2] There was some attempt to penetrate this matter of versions in the debate on 5 July 1979, and I (who had produced many myself on the back of an envelope in the train from the original Greek) had to use some skilful footwork on the platform of Synod. I would still defend them. And in any case Synod has now authorized them, and they are not mine but Synod's. And no application for use of copyright material to anyone has had to be made—they belong in this respect to the Registrar of Synod. See also footnote 4 on page 11 above.

[3] This principle should be emphasized. The Commission may well have got the application of it wrong, but it was this principle (modified by some concern for the best translation) which was the basis.

[4] It is an important pastoral point that congregations which have Bibles should continue to recognize Bibles *as* Bibles, and not think of the 'Word' as solely collections of three readings from Old Testament, Epistles, and Gospels, round a loose theme . . .

[5] See page 13 above.

[6] See Booklet 14C, p.20.

whole. There had been a few psalms released by their inclusion as canticles in various Series 3 services, and more in *Twenty-Five Psalms from a Modern Liturgical Psalter* (C.I.O., 1973). The project was picked up by Collins Liturgical Publications.[1] In fact the whole Psalter first saw light of day when published in June 1977 in the draft of *An Australian Prayer Book,* due to go to the General Synod of the Church of England in Australia in August 1977. In England the Psalter was published by Collins as a separate book on 26 September 1977—*The Psalms—A New Translation for Worship.* This Psalter was approved in July 1978 under the Versions of the Bible Measure for use in public worship. However, when the Synod voted immediately after this authorization on whether to include it in the ASB, the motion was defeated by 195 votes to 126.[2] The rules of Synod would not permit the matter to be raised again for another year.

In the debate on 'progress' report on the ASB on 4 July 1979, the Bishop of Durham moved a motion 'That this Synod considers that the Alternative Service Book should contain a version of the Psalms'. He accepted an amendment that inserted the words 'the standard edition of'. Then Prebendary Michael Baughen (now Bishop of Chester) moved an amendment to omit the last six words and insert instead 'be produced in two versions, one containing a psalter and one not containing a psalter'. The Bishop of Durham spoke of the implication being a breaking of contracts with the publishers.[3] But the Synod carried the amendment by 104 votes to 96, and then carried the amended motion easily on a show of hands.

This left open the question of *which* psalter should be used. On 7 and 8 November a further 'progress' debate included consideration of a motion introduced by the Bishop of London (Bishop Gerald Ellison), 'That this Synod would welcome inclusion of the Revised Psalter in the standard edition of the Alternative Service Book.' It was well known that the Archbishop of Canterbury (Archbishop Donald Coggan), who, twenty years earlier, had chaired the commission which produced the Revised Psalter, favoured this motion.

However, it had been officially arranged to try the mind of Synod by having an amendment ready to substitute 'Liturgical Psalter' for 'Revised Psalter'—and to balance the arguments of Synod by having York ready to refute London and Canterbury. London acknowledged the desire of Synod for the ASB consistently to address God as 'you' (but thought the Revised Psalter could be easily doctored). Canterbury extolled the Revised Psalter, and thought the 'thou' form no problem. York, acknowledging that it was only one day prior to Canterbury's valedictory from the Synod, offered to have one copy of the ASB bound at his own expense with the Revised Psalter, which he would then present to Canterbury, if Canterbury would let all the others contain the Liturgical Psalter! The amendment and the amended motion were duly carried, and the 'with-Psalter' version of the ASB contains the Liturgical Psalter.

---

1 The whole story is delightfully told by David Frost, the English scholar who took final responsibility for the version, in his Liturgical Study no. 25, *Making the Liturgical Psalter* (Grove Books, 1981).

2 See Booklet 14C, p.8.

3 However, it is doubtful whether the contracts could have been in very precise state at that time, and the Synod was certainly unbothered about it.

5. THE ALTERNATIVE SERVICE BOOK— AUTHORIZATION AND PRODUCTION

The previous chapters have shown how by revision, adaptation, *Miscellaneous Proposals,* and non-legislative provision, the working party and the Synod from February 1976 to November 1979 were bringing the contents of the ASB up to the starting-line. The Bishop of Durham brought a 'Progress Report' (GS 413 dated May 1979) to the July 1979 and November 1979 sessions of General Synod, and some of the debates mentioned in the last chapter grew out of this. The report revealed that three consortia would publish the pew edition, and that Eyre and Spottiswoode, the Queen's Printers, would publish the 'Altar Edition'.[1] It noted the dropping of the Catechism from the contents in 1977, and announced that only one edition of the ASB was now being planned, i.e. one which would include the readings *in extenso*.[2] 'Separates' would now be published, starting soon after the ASB itself would come out.[3] Other services would have their licences extended. And parishes would be given permission for their own printings of copyright material, under the aegis of the Registrar of Synod. Other matters covered the timetable still to be achieved in the July and November sessions (concerning which the fate of a Psalter was a big issue), the actual date of publication of the ASB (for which 1 November 1980 was still intended)[4], and an appendix on finance with some (unduly optimistic) forecasts of prices.

The final stages of authorization came on 8 and 9 November 1979. On the first day the various services to be in the Book, as amended, adapted, and altered by *Miscellaneous Liturgical Proposals*, were listed together to be subject to a single vote, on the following motion:

> 'That Provisional Approval be given to the proposed authorization of the following services and other material for a period of use commencing on the date of publication of the Alternatine Service Book and ending on 31 December 1990.'

The list of contents followed, and the motion was carried easily on a show of hands.

The next day the pantechnicon motion came for Final Approval. The Bishop of Durham moved the motion in the following form:

> 'That Final Approval by given to the proposed authorization of the following services and other material for a period of use commencing on the date of the

---

[1] The title 'Altar' edition later ran into trouble, as the Church of England's formularies have never used this word (for obvious reasons). But the title is the title, and its use here involves no value judgments.

[2] See page 18 above. No psalter was in view in May 1979.

[3] This announcement unleashed some relief, as in July 1978 the message the Bishop of Durham conveyed was that it would be necessary to 'restrict' publication of 'separates'. The speech of Brian Brindley in Synod on the matter on 4 July 1979 is well worth reading . . .

[4] It was this discussion (which depended, as far as the report was concerned, on the ability of Synod to keep to its tight timetable) which led to the extension of periods of existing authorization to 'the date of the publication of the Alternative Service Book' and to the authorizing of ASB services *from* that (technically unknown) date.

publication of the Alternative Service Book and ending on 31 December 1990:

	As amended by:	As adapted by:
SERIES 1 and 2 REVISED:		
Holy Communion (AS 217)	GS 405A[1]	GS 380, 380A
SERIES 3:		
Morning and Evening Prayer (AS 310)	GS 405, 405A, 405B	GS 362, 362A
Collects (AS 302)	GS 405, 405A	GS 380, 380A
Initiation Services (AS 330)	GS 405A	GS 393, 393A
The Marriage Service (AS 350)	GS 405A	GS 380, 380A
Funeral Services (AS 360)	GS 405A	GS 360, 362A
Ordination Services	GS 405A	GS 380, 380A
SERIES 3 REVISED:		
The Order for Holy Communion (GS 364F, 364G)	GS 364H, 405A, 405B	
MISCELLANEOUS:		
Alternative Calendar, Rules to Order the Service, and Lectionary (GS 292B, 292C)	GS 365, 365A, 405, 405A	GS 393, 393A'

The voting was as follows:

	Ayes	Noes
Bishops	13	0
Clergy	107	1
Laity	105	2

Thus the synodical programme was triumphantly brought to a close, and the publishing process set in hand.[2]

With the exception noted in footnote 2 below, the ASB and its services do not then reappear on the Synod agenda in February and July 1980. Instead, the secretary-general released on 23 April 1980 a 'fact sheet', circulated by the Liturgical Commission, but not noticeably in other ways connected with it. This sheet answered various questions in people's minds, and the following paragraph is based upon it.

The Book was now to be published on not 1 November, but, 10 November 1980.[3] There would be pew editions with and without the Psalter, and in a variety of bindings, from the three sets of publishers—Cambridge, Clowes, SPCK; Oxford, Mowbray; Hodder and Stoughton. Pagination would be identical in each. Other information in the 'fact sheet' concerned

[1] The accounts above mention 'GS 405' etc., and the form 'GS 405A' (etc.) means the report consolidating amendments made during revision to the original report.

[2] There *was* one 'following motion' left over from the 'progress' debates. On 10 July 1980 Brian Brindley was at last called to move 'That this Synod considers that an edition of the Alternative Service Book without Psalms and Ordination Services (and, if practicable, without Readings for Holy Communion) should be published simultaneously (or nearly so) with the full edition.' The motion was defeated on a show of hands.

[3] The reasons never fully emerged, but perhaps, as the time drew near, someone spotted that the chosen date, 1 November, was a *Saturday*! Once the move to the following Monday had been conceded, it seemed sense to wait a further week, and have it come out at the beginning of the week in which the newly elected Synod would assemble, and be addressed by the Queen. Mondays are good for Church press business, and give the shops a clear starting-point.

the role and status of 1662 and of other authorized services; the responsibilities of the incumbent and PCC, and the prospect of separate printings of individual services. There was also mention of a Commentary on the ASB on which the Liturgical Commission was working.

The first signs of the coming of the Book to worshippers generally were the publication of Rite A in its separate format on 1 May 1980, and growing advance publicity in the early Autumn—headed by the phrase 'The Greatest Publishing Event in the Church of England since 1662'. There were also kind remarks for the Liturgical Commission, and its Chairman, Dean Ronald Jasper, in the first presidential address of the new Archbishop of Canterbury, Robert Runcie, when he spoke on 8 July.[1]

The pew edition of the Book was duly published on 10 November, with a variety of special offers and discounts for quantities.[2] The press responded in various ways—*The Times,* for instance, being apparently unaware the event had happened. On 12 November the new Synod convened, and the Queen addressed it, making reference to the ASB in her first paragraph (including '. . . the Synod may be glad to have some relief from liturgical business'). The Archbishop of York presented her with a copy of the Book, saying he would have liked to have given her a copy of the BCP to match it ('But, your Majesty, I presume you already have a copy . . .'). The following Sunday, 16 November, a Pastoral Letter from the two Archbishops was read in every pulpit in the Church of England.[3]

The Altar Edition was published a few days late, and encountered some criticism for having Rite A and Rite B first, and then the propers *in extenso* (all non-eucharistic materials were excluded). This meant that it was difficult to persuade to remain flat for the regular use of Rite A, and the critics thought the Rites themselves should have been at the centre of the Book. The pew edition was criticized for its part for its minute page numbers.[4] A 'Desk Edition' was added to the range in 1982, and a wholly new pew edition in July 1984.[5] The latter increased the size of those page numbers. Since 1980 most of the main services have appeared as offprinted 'separates'.

At the time of writing the Liturgical Commission is beginning to look towards the needs of the Church of England beyond 31 December 1990. This is by no means premature.

[1] '. . . . I want to pay a special tribute to the Dean of York . . . who has held together so lively a team and put his own considerable liturgical scholarship totally at the service of the Commission, of this Synod, and of the Church . . . he has been the director of the enterprise . . .' (Grove Books got a kind mention too in this end-of-term bouquet . . .).

[2] The Liturgical Commission's *A Commentary on the Alternative Service Book* (C.I.O.) was published the same day.

[3] This Pastoral Letter is reprinted as Appendix A on the inside front cover.

[4] The versions in paperback, and those without psalter, did not sell well.

[5] The Desk Edition sorted out for the first time the massive wrong printing on pages 954-957, and added a tendentious, almost self-congratulatory, note on page 978. The new pew edition, whilst it has eliminated around 60 printing (or rather proof-reading) errors in the 1980 edition, has added a few new ones of its own!

6. EXISTING AUTHORIZED ALTERNATIVE SERVICES

GS 413, the last 'Progress Report' to Synod on the ASB, dated May 1979, listed in its Appendix 2 various services in Series 1, 2, and 3 which were authorized until 31 December 1979. In July 1979, in the debate on the report, the Bishop of Durham moved that provisional approval be given 'to the proposed extension of the period of use of the alternative services listed in Appendix 2 of GS 413 until the date of the publication of the Alternative Service Book'. This was carried without debate. On 7 November final approval followed.[1] The services thus extended included, as will appear below, those to be authorized in adapted form in the ASB, those to be renewed as booklets, and those to cease from authorization.

(a) Those to go into the ASB in adapted form
These were all listed in the motion on the contents of the ASB on page 21 above, The unadapted forms were not renewed beyond the date of publication of the ASB.

(b) Those to have an extended licence in booklet form
The Standing Committee brought a report before Synod in July 1980, GS 439, which recommended a sparing renewal of licences for an 'intermediate' set of services. These were:

> Series 1 Matrimony; Series 1 Burial of the Dead.
> Series 2 Holy Communion; Series 2 Baptism and Confirmation.
> Series 2 Revised Morning and Evening Prayer; Series 3 Holy Communion.

The last two of these were to be shorn of their appended tables of Psalms and Lessons. The intention was to give one 'intermediate service for each kind of rite—Series 2 where available, Series 1 where not. The 'run on' of Series 3 Communion (the green booklet) was a natural addition to the list. These duly gained provisional approval on 9 July 1980, after various attempts to extend or reduce the list had been beaten off. Later the same week, on 11 July 1980, the services received final approval or the extension of their licence to 31 December 1985.[2]

(c) Services which lapsed when the ASB was published
The remaining services listed in GS 413, which had no renewal of their licence, were as follows:

> Series 1: Baptism, Litany, Quicunque Vult, Holy Communion.

In the debate of 9 July 1980 mentioned above, when various services had their period extended, attempts were made to include Series 1 Communion (the amendment was lost by 148-104) and Series 1 Baptism (the amendment was lost easily.) An attempt to resurrect Series 1 Morning and Evening Prayer which had lapsed in 1973 was withdrawn.

Other bits and pieces
There were two other bits and pieces worth mentioning. One was the Revised Catechism. It had originally been scheduled for inclusion in the

---

[1] The voting was: Bishops 31-0; Clergy 165-0; Laity 150-0.
[2] The voting was: Bishops 20-0; Clergy 106-3; Laity 123-5.

ASB, but had been dropped by the working party. Instead it was separately 'commended' for use in instruction until 31 December 1985, gaining provisional approval on 8 November 1979. This returned and gained final approval on 7 July 1980.[1] The other was a rationalization of existing lectionaries and rules to order the service. There was provision attached to various services in booklet form which in totality gave too much choice, and an apparent lack of principle, to the official provision. Thus the Liturgical Commission brought forward a report (GS 427, which was to be read with GS (Misc) 117) to rationalize these provisions, and in particular to bring them all within a slightly expanded 'Prayer Book' choice of material which makes up one complete and self-consistent lectionary for the Prayer Book Church year.[2] The report was received and its recommendation endorsed by Synod on 7 November 1979, and a firms set of 'Proposals for Rationalization of Tables and Lessons, Psalms and Rules to Order the Service (GS 440)' came back on 9 July 1980. They were given general consideration, revision in full synod, and provisional approval that day. Then on 11 July 1980 they received final approval, for 'a period beginning on the date of the publication of the Alternative Service Book and ending on 31 December 1985'.[3]

Since 1980

In the years that followed there were various discussions on the new Liturgical Commission as to whether a Series 1 Communion service, or some similar device which allowed common deviations from the 1662 Communion service, should not be re-introduced. However, the general view of the Commission was that minor variations should be viewed as simply falling under the ministerial discretion allowed in the Canons[4], and forms running nearer to Series 1 were in fact obtainable within the rather hybrid Rite B. Finally, the House of Bishops took independent action, contrary to the advice of the Liturgical Commission. The minutes of their meeting on 18 October 1983 showed that they intended to bring a motion to Synod. On 29 February 1984 the Bishop of Birmingham (Hugh Montefiore) moved 'That the Synod requests the House of Bishops to introduce into the Synod at the next group of sessions (a) the text of Series 1 Baptism Service and (b) the text of Series 1 Holy Communion Service

[1] The voting was: Bishops 21-1; Clergy 98-15; Laity 95-16.

[2] The Prayer Book Calendar is not identical to the Alternative Calendar in the ASB. The semi-official annual *Almanack* (Mowbray/SPCK) puts the Prayer Book provision on the left-hand page facing the ASB provision (though separate booklets of each are also available). This provision clearly belongs with the left-hand page material.

[3] The voting was: Bishops 25-0; Clergy 123-0; Laity 134-1.

[4] This point was rather made for the Commission, and indeed made more strongly than the Registrar of Synof could have wished, we think, when Eyre and Spottiswoode, the Queen's Printers, the guardians of the copyright of the 1662 BCP, in late 1983 produced their own attractive booklet entitled *Holy Communion According to the Book of Common Prayer (1662) with minor variations*, and defended the departure from the official text (e.g. by the inclusion of the Lord's Summary of the Law, and the exclusion of long exhortations) by citing the principle of 'minor variations' from Canon B5. In Synod one or two questioners tried on occasions to get the Archbishop of Canterbury to rule that this or that practice was merely a 'minor variation', but no-one expected an official text from the most impeccable quarters to produce cavalier alterations in this way.

so that they can be considered for authorization under Canon B2.' An amendment tacked in Series 1 Morning and Evening Prayer (which had been defunct since 1973) also. But Synod was restive. An attempt to have the question 'not put' was only defeated by 179 votes to 149, and at the end of the day the voting was: Bishops 28-1; Clergy 122-66; Laity 91-80. The House of Bishops did not bring the proposal back at the next session, and at the time of writing they seem unlikely to try it in November 1984. Not only would there by little likelihood of the requisite two-thirds majority in each House for authorization, but in additiion they have done some careful work, previously overlooked, on Rite B, and discovered most of what they want is available in the 'Series 1' part of the options therein![1]

At the time of writing Synod will soon have to take decisions about the extending, or not extending, the period of authorization of the existing services which were licensed up to 31 December 1985. It seems possible that Series 2 and Series 3 Communion services will not be reintroduced, but the other services will be. Periaps the Revised Catechism deserves a harder look in 1985 than it received in 1980.

---

[1] Indeed there is a prospect of a semi-official printing of 'Rite B with choice of material most carefully calculated to persuade Series 1 lovers that they are getting just what they wanted'!

7 BACKLASH

This chapter stands out of a logical sequence with the others. It records virtually nothing official. But a history of the period concerned would have been defective without it. The difficulty is that the two sides in the particular controversy differ as to how important an issue it is. Here we compromise and give it a passing mention.

The 'backlash' is that of the lovers of Prayer Book English. Although the arguments about a modern style of English were largely conducted on the world's liturgical commissions and committees between 1966 and 1973, and although the first texts of the Church of England's Commission, *Modern Liturgical Texts*, were published in 1968, the backlash against modern English in the liturgy did not really gather force until around 1978, which was perhaps ten years too late, and thus exposed the movement to great frustration as they were unable to make much difference to official policy.

Whilst mutterings and grumblings occurred in the press throughout the 1970s, the first signs of a concerted attack were occasional articles by Professor David Martin in *The Daily Telegraph* around 1977 and 1978. Then, at the November 1979 session of General Synod, when all the ASB services were to get final approval in order to set the publishing programme in hand' the chairman of the House of Laity, Mr. Oswald Clark, presented to the Synod (as he had under standing orders the right to do) a Petition signed by 600 eminent persons, asking for the BCP and the AV to have a fair innings in the liturgical future. The Petition was contained for the general public within a journal *PN Review* 13[1], the particular edition of which had David Martin as its guest editor and 'Crisis for Cranmer and King James' as its title. Article after article by the literati and the dons attack the modern services and their 'imposition' by the clergy on an unwilling laity. Finally come the Petitions themselves—the first and great one, signed by the 600, 'deeply concerned by the policies and tendencies which decree the loss of both the Authorized Version of the bible and the Book of Common Prayer'; the second one milder, and signed by fewer, merely 'concerned for' the AV and the BCP; and the third, 'The Saint Cecilia Petition, supporting traditional texts and their accompanying music, and signed by musicians, including a good number of cathedral organists and directors of music. *PN Review* 13 did not figure on the Synod agenda and never has since. One speech was made against it in the passing in the debate on final approval of Rite A on 7 November 1979, but that was a deliberate excursus for the sake of the record.[2]

---

[1] The cryptic title apparently means *'Poetry Nation Review'*. The '13' is unexplained, as the issue was volume 6 number 5. The journal acknowledges financial support from the Arts Council!

[2] Michael Saward made a speech to this particular gallery, suggesting that the unbelieving non-worshipping persons who want the ancient literature to be in use should hire halls and have public readings of the BCP and AV.

[3] The point here is that Parliament was proposing to over-rule powers given to Synod, and thus provoke a clash between the law of the land and the Canons of the Church of England—or alternatively, a missive *to* Synod would have required Synod to change the Canons, which would have been a highly provocative step.

Since that time the backlash has continued. The national press has at intervals echoed the charge that the clergy are robbing the laity of their due. There have been two gallup polls, one in the archdeaconry of Chichester, one on the streets of Birmingham. There have been Commons' motions, *Times* leaders, and public meetings galore. There have been three symposia wholly or largely devoted to attacking the ASB: Brian Morris (ed.) *Ritual Murder* (Carcanet Press, Manchester, 1980); David Martin and Peter Mullen (eds.) *No Alternative: The Prayer Book Controversy* (Blackwell, 1981); and A. Kilminster (ed.) *When Will Ye Be Wise? The State of the Church of England* (Blond and Briggs, 1983). The nearest approach to sympathy the General Synod has shown was through a question about the liturgical uses at the theological colleges, tabled at the February 1981 session. The answer showed great affection for Rite A, very little for Rite B, and not vastly more than that for 1662. This gave fuel to the next public event.

On 8 April 1981 Lord Sudeley introduced in the House of Lords, and Viscount Cranbourne had ten minutes in the Commons to 'seek leave to introduce', a draft bill entitled 'The Prayer Book Protection Bill'. The bill would have accorded to any 20 persons on a parish electoral roll the right to insist on a 1662 service as the main morning service once a month. The force of such a bill was not only to allow a tiny proportion of persons—perhaps only occasional worshippers—to overrule the patterns of worship of perhaps hundreds of people, and to frustrate the decisions of their representatives on the Parochial Church Councils, but also to invade the powers conferred on General Synod by the Church of England (Worship and Doctrine) Measure 1974, and thus provoke a constitutional crisis between church and state.[1] The government thus properly resisted the bill—but its supporters carried it by 152 votes to 130 in the Commons and 24 to 12 in the Lords. The result heartened the 'Prayer Book lobby' no end, though the bill itself did not receive parliamentary time and thus collapsed when the parliamentary session ended in July 1981. The bishops in the House of Bishops decided on a threefold action:

(i) to discuss liturgical uses with their Bishops' Councils
(ii) to ask the standing committee of General Synod to prepare another edition of the parish *Guide* to the Worship and Doctrine Measure
(iii) to ask 'that Governing Bodies and Principles [of theological colleges] pay attention to this matter with a view to ensuring the use both of the Book of Common Prayer and the Alternative Service Prayer Book in teaching and in worship'.[2]

What the bishops could not do, and did not do, was to diminish the power of choice of services residing with incumbents and PCCs in each parish, which could well (as a theoretical position) result in *no* parishes using the BCP at all.

---

[1] A crisis because statute Law would have been at odds with Canon Law, and the Clergy could not have known which to obey.

[2] The quotation is from the letter sent on behalf of the House of Bishops to the colleges on 3 July 1981. The colleges were always the whipping-boy in this exercise—it was the wicked brainwashing in the chapel and in the class room which meant that the 'young men' were not content to allow 1662 to run on in the parishes! The questions begged by this analysis are legion.

Lord Sudeley was not satisfied, as indeed he could not be. Thus on 11 April 1984, he moved again a (slightly altered) version of the same bill. This time he had a harder passage. The bishops turned up in greater numbers, though their opposition to the bill was made in the tactical form '1662 is alive and well all round the country—why do we need such legislation?'—a tactic which sounds like special pleading on the one hand, and a failure to get the supporters of the bill to come to terms with a changing church on the other. Lord Hailsham, the Lord Chancellor, rose from the Woolsack, and dismembered the bill piece by piece as unworkable and unworthy legislation. Lord Sudeley withdrew it.

The account above does indicate one danger point. In the 1974 debate in the House of Lords on the Worship and Doctrine Measure, the bishops managed to convey the impression that keeping the BCP 'available' (to use the word in the Measure) would mean it was in general use. This of course could not be guaranteed by the Measure or the bishops, and for those who looked at the clause it was clear it would find its own level, and in particular would be affected by the publication of the ASB. It is currently finding that level, and the level does drop each year, and may one year cease altogether. It may not 'be desirable' that the BCP is doomed, but it is inevitable, and the bishops would do better to admit it.

8 SERVICES FOR THE SICK AND KINDRED AFFAIRS

The Liturgical Commission in the 1970s pleaded itself too busy to tackle the visitation and communion of the sick. In 1965, the original *'First Series'* report from the Houss of Bishops had carried a final page with the words 'VIII. AN ORDER FOR THE COMMUNION OF THE SICK' and under the title *'A form of service and rubrics are under consideration'*. However, nothing emerged ever. The problem of the reservation of the sacramental elements loomed large over the issue, and it was acknowledged in the original list of contents of the ASB in February 1976 that no services for use with the sick would be in the Book.[1] However, when the last major report from the Commission in preparation fot rhe ASB, namely the revised text of Series 3 communion, published as GS 364 in May 1978, had left the Commission's hands, there remained some time and energy for the Commission to work on the omitted material.[2]

The central service for use with the sick was bound to be the communion of the sick. On this the Commission found a way to agree (subject to a dissent noted below) about communion 'by extension'—i.e. that clergy, and lay distributants also, should go from a full eucharistic liturgy with consecrated elements which they would take to the sick in their homes or elsewhere. The question of 'reserving' for a space of time was simply not touched, though clearly it was not now forbidden.[3] Thus the Commission could provide both for a full rite at a bedside, and also for this satellite rite.

However, there were two side issues which proved in the event to be contentious. One was the 'Reconciliation of a Penitent'. The Commission insisted that this should contain the clause 'I absolve you from all your sins', and the rite should not simply come in the context of the visiting of the dying (as in the BCP) but should be a general provision for the physically healthy as well as the sick. This, to my mind, meant that the rite ceased to be 'alternative' to anything in the BCP, and could not appeal tp precedent in the BCP. And the *'ego absolvo te'*, even though carefully qualified by its verbal context, I thought to be theologically improper. It proved to be non-negotiable for the majority, which *increased* the theological problem. In early 1980 I was invited to send a memorandum to the House of Bishops about my opposition to this, but the memorandum was rejected, and I was driven into dissent.

The other side issue was the 'blessing of the oils'. The Calendar and Lectionary revision process in 1977 and 1978 had led to the inclusion in the ASB of provision for 'The Blessing of the Oils' on Maundy Thursday, with a full set of propers on pages 555-557—saving only that there were no prayers for the actual 'blessing' of the oils. Services for the sick were a natural context in which to provide for the blessing of oil for anointing the sick, which, after the eucharistic provision, was one of the main tasks the Commission had had to address. Furthermore, Canon B37 had for many years required

---

1 See Booklet 14B page 12.

2 The Commission's own life was due to run to 20 February 1981; see Booklet 13B page 6

3 The rubric after communion (as e.g., in rite A no. 49) prescribes consumption during the service or after it is over for elements *'not required for purposes of communion'*. This would mean that reservation should have no other end in view but administration to those absent from a celebration.

that oil for anointing the sick should be so blessed. The Commission was aware that those who wished to anoint baptismal and confirmation candidates also wanted their oils blessed, and in many cases wanted this to happen on Maundy Thursday under the presidency of the diocesan bishop in his own cathedral (hence the propers in the ASB). So the Commission had here (as with 'Reconciliation') a task wider than a ministry to the sick.

The upshot was that the Commission produced two documents. The first was *Services for the Sick*, including two orders for communion of the sick, provision for laying on of hands and anointing, prayers for use with the dying, and an appendix of various prayers for various occasions. The second was *The Blessing of the Oils and The Reconciliation of a Penitent* (GS 472). The Commission finished these in May 1980. One member of the Commission, Hugh Craig, dissented from the whole set of reports, whilst I dissented from the absolution in the 'Reconciliation' rite. The two reports were published (after a lengthy delay) in December 1890. All of them received 'general consideration' on 5 July 1981, in what were technically two separate debates, introduced by Donald Gray, the chairman of the Steering Committee. They were then referred to a common Revision Committee. under the well-tried chairmanship of the Bishop of Derby[2], and amendments were sent in, or moved in person, by members of Synod. In the Revision Committee GS 472 was divided into two separate entities, so that it became clear that three separate sets would be presented to Synod for the Revision stages. The Committee, well suffused with well-meant suggestions, sat from September 1981 to May 1982, and reported to General Synod with a single introduction to the revision of three separate texts (GS 471A, GS 472A (Blessing of oils), and GS 530 (Reconciliation)) on 6 July 1982. After this, the three entities can best be treated under their separate headings.

(a) **Ministry to the sick**

The Revision Committee changed the title of these services to *Ministry to the Sick*. Most of the actual revision was done in the Committee, and little of importance occurred in the Synod. The pattern of the provision emerged as follows:

> (i) **Communion with the Sick:**
> Notes
> A Form of Personal Preparation
> The celebration of the Holy Communion in the presence of the Sick ('Rite A' and 'Rite B' forms)
> The Distribution of Communion to those not present at a Celebration[3]. ('Rite A' and 'Rite B' forms)

---

[1] The note in GS 472 ran as follows: '. . . two members of the commission, the Revd. C. O. Buchanan and Mr. H. R. M. Craig, wish to dissociate themselves from this provision [i.e. of two absolutions, one in the 'I absolve you' form] for doctrinal reasons. They would wish that all the alternatives provided for absolution should be acceptable to all the main sections of the Church of England; and they do not believe that the indicative formula—"I absolve you from all sins"—falls into this category.'

[2] It was he who chaired the Revision Committee on Rite A (see page 6 above). The procedures for Revision Committee and Revision Stage in full Synod are set out in Booklet 14A, page 13.

[3] This title had replaced 'extension' and its cognates.

(ii) **The Laying on of Hands with Prayer, and Anointing**
    Notes
    The Laying on of Hands with Prayer, and Anointing
        (at Holy Communion, and at Morning or Evening Prayer, and
        on their own)
(iii) **A Commendation at the Time of Death**
(iv) **Prayers for Use with the Sick**
(Appendix) **Psalms and Readings**

The Revision Stage was held 6 July 1982. and led easily to provisional approval. The services were referred to the House of Bishops, and then came back for final approval on 9 November 1982. The period of authorization was from 1 June 1983 to 31 December 1990, and the voting was:

	Ayes	*Noes*
Bishops	22	0
Clergy	140	2
Laity	123	5

The services were published as a substantial booklet (ASB 70) on 26 May 1983, costing at that time £1.[1] Subsequently a card fot rhe communion of the sick on the one side and the laying on of hands and anointing on the other, each in an abbreviated form, was published as ASB 72.[2] The services will remain separate from the ASB itself (despite the coding shown), but the question of their integration with the book will arise in relation to the post-1990 situation.

(b) The Blessing of the Oils

When the Revision Committee brought GS 472A before the General Synod on 6 July 1982 there was some complaint about the concept of 'blessing oils' in the debate on the Revision Committee's report.[3] However the Revision Stage itself was conducted fairly easily, the most notable event being the addition by an amendment from the floor of a Roman Catholic hymn, *O Redeemer.* There was no text available in the amendment, although one member produced a version from his pocket and read it aloud. The Synod accepted the amendment by 133 voted to 123. The other alterations were minimal in their impact. And the Synod then gave provisional approval on a show of hands.

[1] A fuller account of the background and contents of this provision is to be found in Grove Worship Series no. 84, Colin Buchanan and David Wheaton *Liturgy for the Sick: The New Church of England Services* (Grove Books, 1983).

[2] This card was edited in an unfortunate way, and is distinctly misleading. In particular, the text which the official services contain, as providing the theological 'backdrop' to the distribution to those absent from a celebration, is missing from the card. This text runs as follows, and it was integral to the synodical agreement on the provision:
    The church of God, of which we are members, has taken bread and wine and given thanks over them according to our Lord's command. I bring these holy gifts that you may share in the communion of his body and blood. We who are many are one body, because we all share in onr bread.
The other side of the card, concerning laying on of hands and anointing, does not do much better.

[3] One newly elected member went so far as to call it 'rather like a form of white magic'!

The text was then referred, in accordance with standing orders, to the House of Bishops. Behind the scenes, various members of the Steering Committee indicated that they would be driven into opposition if the Roman Catholic hymn were not deleted, and the original mover of the amendment acknowledged that he would be happy with *'A Suitable hymn may be sung'*, so on 19 October 1982 the House of Bishops made that change.

The texts came to General Synod for final approval on 9 November 1982. The proposal was that they should be authorized from 31 March 1983 (i.e. Maundy Thursday) to 31 December 1990. And suddenly everything went wrong for the materials. Archdeacon Peter Dawes, who had opposed the use of oil in initiation[1], now rose to urge that the Church of England has no theology of the use of oil in such cases, and therefore cannot construct prayers usefully without getting a theology. Alan Bretherton mocked the 'link with the bishop concept'. David Holloway pointed out we had never needed agreed texts to provide oil for use with the sick.[2] Others protested about the London diocesan way of uniting the renewal of ordination vows with this rather sectionalist event, the Maundy Thursday 'blessing of oils'. The Bishop of Birmingham (Hugh Montefiore) pitched in with a point that the Synod was all too eager to 'authorize' that which was already happening quite happily, and did not need official 'authorization'.[3] And in half an hour the provision had diasppeared down the drain.[4] The voting was as follows:

	Ayes	Noes
Bishops	26	6
Clergy	131	49
Laity	101	61

There was no two-thirds majority in the House of Laity, so the provision was *not* finally approved.[5]

(c) The Reconciliation of a Penitent

In the debate on the Revision Committee's report on 6 July 1982, there were enough indications that some members of Synod still had difficulties with the wording 'I absolve you' for it to be clear that GS 530 would not have an easy passage. Its Revision Stage was taken partly that day, partly on 9 July 1982. Three crucial amendments were tabled to excise or alter 'I absolve you'. The first, moved by Jim Duxbury, was voted out by 249 votes to 59, and the next two, moved by me, were voted out without a count being called. I then resigned from the Steering Committee for this rite in order to be able to oppose its further progress. On 9 July the vote for provisional approval was also taken on a show of hands, and the rite was referred to the House of Bishops. They fiddled with some secondary wording, but left 'I absolve you' untouched.

[1] See page 5 above.

[2] In other words, the requirementsof canon B 37 had never had a text attached before.

[3] And , of course, because these prayers were not 'alternative' to any material in the BCP, they did *not* need authorization.

[4] There was another factor which may have borne upon the issue. As shown below, the controversial rite for 'The Reconciliation of a Penitent' was on the agenda to follow the 'blessing of the oils'. In the event it was taken off at the last minute. So there may have been some hostility to *that* rite in members of Synod, which ,if that rite had still been on the agenda, would have been saved up for it.i But then event it was unleashed on the poor unfortunate 'blessing of the oils'!

[5] Impartial as always, *News of Liturgy* published the text immediately, and it can of course be used, as it never needed authorization.

In November 1982, this rite was on the agenda for its 'Final Approval' stage, which would have followed immediately after the Ministry to the Sick, and the Blessing of the Oils, debates. However, at the beginning of the session, the secretary-general announced that the chairman and vice-chairman of Laity had asked, as they had the constitutional right to do, for the Reconciliation of a Penitent to be referred to separate Houses.[1] This took the rite off the November 1982 agenda, and the debating in separate Houses came prior to the meeting of the full Synod in February 1983. The voting on a simple motion to approve the rite, on 7 February 1983, was as follows:

		Ayes	*Noes*
Canterbury—Bishops		25	2
	Clergy	96	23
York	—Bishops	7	3
	Clergy	42	15
House of Laity		96	55

The York Convocation (Bishops and Clergy together) defeated my motion 'That this Convocation does not believe that official authorization is necessary for the use of the proposed "Reconciliation" Rite'[2] by 33 to 32.

As the 'separate reference' had not obstructed the passage of the rite (though it *had* revealed that it might lack a two-thirds majority in the House of Laity), it came back to the Synod for Final Approval on 8 February 1983. The Bishop of Birmingham this time emerged as a fierce *proponent* of 'authorizing' that which it is not necessary to authorize in Synod.[3] Various persons, including me, opposed him. An attempt was made (as it had been made in the Convocation of York the previous day) to adjourn the debate without a decision, but this was lost. The motion, for authorization from 1 June 1983 to 31 December 1990, was voted on as follows:

	Ayes	*Noes*
Bishops	35	6
Clergy	157	49
Laity	124	75

Authorization was not granted, as the House of Laity had not given a two-thirds vote in favour.[4]

[1] This actually means 'to the separate Houses of the two Convocations of the Clergy and to the House of Laity'—*five* Houses in all. This was a defensive position built in to the original Synodical Government Measure in 1969, but, until this event, it had never previously been invoked. Most of the proceedings in the five Houses had in fact all the allure of a non-event, though the count in the Laity had its own interest.

[2] The motion was a desirable background to my opposition to authorizing the service. It was, however, made all the pointed by the fact that the Registrar of Synod, Mr. Brian Hanson, provided his response to my motion by compiling a 'Legal Opinion' (which was then deposited on the chairs of members of the five Houses debating on 7 February) opposing the thrust of the motion. The 'Legal Opinion' expounded (on transparently thin evidence) the view that this 'Reconciliation' rite was an 'alternattive' to the provision for those *in articulo mortis* in the BCP, and therefore needed to be authorized. (This would also have had the paradoxical effect that only the 1662 form (with enquiry as to whether the sick person had made his or her will!) could be used until such time as the new rite was passed. No one ever took it too seriously, but it might be viewed at the time as putting extra pressure upon members of Synod to pass the rite, lest they be 'depriving' others of what they wanted if they did not.

[3] We know he did not by the following day view it as necessary for the Synod to authorize under Canon B2, as, after it was rejected, he 'authorized' it himself off his own bat for his own diocese under Canon B4!

[4] Once again, *News of Liturgy* came to the rescue and published the text, as that there might be those who wanted to use it in their private ministry on their own authority.

9 CHRISTIAN INITIATION—POLICY QUESTIONS

Several different matters occurred during the period, over and above the provision of the rites in the ASB, as described in chapter 2 above.

(a) Amending of Canon B21

On 8 November 1977 Peter Dawes successfully moved a motion for taking out 'from time to time' from the Canon, and substituting 'normally'.[1] This was then enshrined in draft 'Amending Canon (No. 6)' which was generally approved', without comment on this part of a composite Amending Canon, on 8 July 1978.[2] It was referred to a Revision Committee, and the rest of Canon B 21 was brought into consistency with it. The revised text came to Synod on 6 November 1978, and, without revision in full Synod, it was then agreed that the relevant part 'stand part of the draft Canon', On 9 November 1978, the draft Amending Canon no. 6 was finally approved on a show of hands, and the petition for 'Her Majesty's Royal Assent and Licence to promulge and execute the Canon . . .' was also approved on a show of hands. The Canon was duly promulged, and its effect is to reword Canon B21 as follows:

> 'It is desirable that every minister having a cure of souls shall normally administer the sacrament of Holy Baptism upon Sundays or other Holy Days at or immediately after public worship when the most number of people come together, that the congregation there present may witness the receiving of them that be newly baptized into Christ's Church, and be put in remembrance of their own profession made to God in their baptism.'

It will be noted that the ASB initiation services picked up this *normally* and included it in opening Notes 1 and 7 on page 241.

(b) Reception of Christians from other Churches

The Rev. Colin Scott moved a motion asking for a common form for such 'reception' on 9 July 1980, but he withdrew the motion as he expected it would be overtaken by the Covenant for Unity.

(c) The 'Indiscriminate' Baptism motion

Mr. J. R. Bradshaw's private member's motion tabled after the 1974-1976 initiation debates ran as follows:

> 'That the General Synod adheres to the view that Infant Baptism should continue to be available to the children of all parents who are willing and able to make the requisite promises: and rejects the words "and able" which were inserted after "willing" in its precedecessor's resolution of February 1974.'[3]

This motion slowly gathered sufficient support to be debated, and it was moved on 9 July 1980, and defeated on a show of hands.

---

[1] See booklet 14C pages 14-15.

[2] This was overlooked in Booklet 14C ,and the end of the paragraph at the top of page 15 in that Booklet was incorrect.

[3] The 'predecessor's resolution' is described in Booklet 14A, page 11. The relevance of Mr. Bradshaw's motion to the Southwell diocesan one which General Synod passed in November 1976 is discussed in Booklet 14C, page 14.

(d) Godparents

On 27 February 1981, the Rev. Michael Hodge successfully moved:

> 'That this Synod would welcome an opportunity to debate the role of Godparents and sponsors in Christian Initiation, including their qualifications and selection, and to this end asks the Standing Committee to prepare and present a Report which will be both theological and practical'.

It is known that the Standing Committee asked the Bishop of Leicester to prepare this report, but at the time of writing it has not been published.

(e) Admission of Children to Communion

After the rejection by General Synod of the principle of admission to communion before the age of discretion in July 1976[1], there was a varied response in the country. In just over one-third of the dioceses the bishops 'winked' at 'experiments'; in another third the bishops would have been sympathetic to such moves, but thought it improper to connive at action which General Synod had rejected; and in the last third the bishops were themselves opposed to any such changes.[2] In the diocese of Winchester a motion was brought to the diocesan Synod asking that General Synod should 'review' the 1976 decision, and 'in the light of the growing demand for such an option, urges the General Synod to permit the introduction of this change in certain dioceses for a period of twelve years as a pilot experiment'.

The diocesan motion was on the agenda of General Synod from 1981 onwards without being reached. Early in 1982 the Board of Educarion, through its 'Committee 2', set up a small working party under the chairmanship of the Bishop of Knaresborough (John Denis) to examine the issues involvee, and to prepare for the General Synod debated.[3]

The Winchester motion was finally debated on 8 February 1983. It was moved by Robert Teare. Michael Hodge moved the deletion of all the words quoted in inverted commas a few lines above (on the formal grounds that we have no reliable knowledge of a 'growing demand'), and succeeded with this by 143 votes to 124. This left the motion in the following form:

> 'That this Synod requests the Standing Committee to review the General Synod's Resolution of July 1976 disallowing the admission of baptized persons to the Holy Communion followed at a later stage by Confirmation.'

This was then carried by 228 votes to 104. The Standing Committee asked the Board of Education to retain the responsibility for the requisite work, and the Board expanded and altered the Knaresborough working party to conduct this 'review'. It was, however, early 1984 before the new working party met, and it will hardly report before Autumn 1985. Meanwhile, the 'conniving' increases.

1 See Booklet 14B, pages 14-15; also Grove Worship Series no. 85, Daniel Young *Welcoming Children to Communion* (Grove Books, 1983), pages 7-8, and Grove Liturgical Study no. 27, David Holeton *Infant Communion-Then and Now* (Grove Books, 1981), pages 29-31.

2 Perhaps it should be noted that there were two distinguishable practices at issue: one was an admission to communion in, say, the last two years of preparation for confirmationation, e.g. at the age of 10 or 11; the other was wholly divorced from confirmation, and could mean the admission of five-year-olds, or even, to go the logical extreme, of babes in arms. In the latter case, the age of confirmation could rise.

3 Another task the original working party gave itself was to set up a consultation for one day in London in June 1983, i.e. after the passing of the 'review' motion in Synod.

10 THE NEW LITURGICAL COMMISSION

Liturgical Commissions nowadays take their lifespan from the quinquennium of each General Synod. Romald Jasper announced in advance that he intended to resign as chairman when the last Commission reached the end of its period on 28 February 1981, and, because of the whole change of era implied by the introduction of the ASB, it became natural to think in terms of a new Commission to be appointed following the election of a new General Synod in Autumn 1980. The old Commission had a farewell dinner at their last meeting on 9 September 1980, and the (then new) Archbishop of Canterbury came along to pay tribute to the retiring chairman.

The new Commission was appointed in Spring 1981, and the names published on 12 June that year. The chairman was the Rev. Professor Douglas Jones, who had previously been Prolocutor of the Lower House of the Convocation of York, and had chaired the Revision Committee on the ordination services in 1977, and taken a leading role in the debates in Synod on the Lord's Prayer and on the Psalter. He had retired from the General Synod, but now was needed back, and the York Convocation soon after co-opted him (as they had done Ronald Jasper in 1975) in order to seat him on Synod. Five of the old Commission returned, four of them General Synod members[1], and another nine names were added. The Rev. Michael Perham served as a 'consultant', being secretary of the Doctrinal Commission and offering a link between the two, and the Commission itself co-opted as a further consultant the Rev. Dr. Geoffrey Cuming. vice-chairman of the previous Commission.

The Commission has worked under less pressure than its predecessor, the natural result of the end of producing the ASB and of the consequential synodical deadlines. Its activities have come into public notice at the following points.

(a) 'Concelebration'

A question asked of the Commission led to its first public statement. Two members, Trevor Lloyd and Hugh Wybrew. produced a brief memorandum on 'concelebration', which was circulated to General Synod members in November 1982 as 'GS (Misc) 163', *Concelebration in the Eucharist*.[3] It has not been debated in Synod.[4]

[1] The four were Colin Buchanan, Donald Gray, Diana McClatchey, and David Silk; the fifth was David Hope.

[2] Its general thrust made it very doubtful whether the Roman Catholic practice of 'Concelebration' had any footing in theology or rubrics in the Church of England.

[3] It would not have been known outside of Synod, had not Grove Books distributed it to Standing Order customer—thus tripling its total circulation! In October 1982 there came a commentary on it, Grove Worship Series no. 82, John Fenwick *Eucharistic Concelebration* (Grove Books, 1982), This reinforced the message of GS (Misc.) 163 not only by its well-argued contents but also through the instant visual impact of Peter Ashton's cartoon cover (q.v.).

[4] The question, had of course, been earlier handled in Synod in connection with the Notes before both the ordination services and Rite A. See Booklet 82 and page 12 above.

(b) The Roman Catholic Three-year Lectionary

After his success with the Daily Eucharistic Lectionary[1], Brian Brindley struck again whilst the iron was hot. He tabled a private member's motion, which, after a long preamble, concluded that the Synod 'asks the House of Bishops, after consultation with the Liturgical Commission, to introduce proposals for the authorization of the three-year lectionary, *mutatis mutandis,* for an experimental period as an optional alternative to existing authorized lectionaries.' He moved this on 9 November 1982, and it was soon after adjourned to 12 November. The Commission had prepared its own amendment which did not tip the scales towards authorization, and the amendment was accepted, and the amended motion was also accepted, on a show of hands. It now read as follows:

> 'That this Synod notes the recommendations in Resolution 24 of the Lambeth Conference, that a common Lectionary should be adopted, and the attention there drawn to the experience of those Provinces which have adopted the three-year Eucharistic lectionary of the Roman Catholic Church; would welcome the opportunity to consider the authorization of the Eucharistic Lectionary of the Roman Catholic Church; and invites the House of Bishops to instruct the Liturgical Commission to prepare a report comparing the provisions of that lectionary with those of the BCP and the Alternative Services.'

The House of Bishops duly instructed the Commission ,and the Commission prepared a report, *A Common Lectionary* (GS 603), published in November 1983. The report set out the full Roman provision for Sundays and Holy Days as an appendix, and weighed the gains and losses in authorizing it as an alternative lectionary for the Church of England. In the chairman's preface to the report he wrote: '. . . it does not advise any particular course of action. Most members of the Commission draw from the analysis [in the report] the conclusion that it will be wise to proceed no further'. When he came to move that 'the Synod do take note of this Report' on 29 February 1984, he followed the same even-handedness. Brian Brindley spoke in favour of authorizing the Roman lectionary, and Donald Gray as a Commission member spoke against it. The debate was adjourned, and there was still Brian Brindley's 'following motion' to come:

> 'That this Synod respectfully requests the House of Bishops to introduce into the Synod at an early opportunity proposals to permit the use in the Church of England, for a period of nine years, subject to the usual safeguards, as an optional alternative use to the presently authorized Tables of Lessons for Holy Communion, of the Three Year Sunday Eucharistic Lectionary referred to in GS 603 (with the minimum of adaptation) together with appropriate psalms and any necessary Alternative Collects, as a step towards the eventual introduction of a Common Lectionary available for use by all English-speaking Christians.'

In July 1984 the item was moved off the agenda by pressure of other business, and at the time of writing it is expected it will come again in November 1984.

[1] See Booklet 14C, pages 21-22, and pages 3 and 13-14 above.

(c) Lent, Holy Week, and Easter

It has been no secret that the Commission has been working on provision for this season, going beyond the relatively sparing material in the BCP and the ASB. At the meeting of diocesan liturgical secretaries on 10 May 1984, the 'wraps' came off the first time, and drafts were discussed (and an 'agape' shared!). The Commission has since touched up the drafts, and at the time of writing they are with the printers and are due for publication (under the title *Lent—Holy Week—Easter*) in late November or early December 1984.

It is intended to authorize these services by a different procedure from that used for services 'alternative' to those in the BCP, which fall under Canon B 2. Instead, they will be authorized by the two archbishops acting under Canon B 4 (2). However, the Synod will have a say in the matter, because the plan is that in February 1985 there will be a general debate on the services as published, and there will also be an opportunity for members of Synod (and others) to send in proposals for amendment to the Commission, The Commission will then amend the text, and forward it to the archbishops for authorization.

(d) Services of Prayer and Dedication after Civil Marriage

Alongside the many diocesan rites of 'Blessing' of civil marriages (which have played a variety of roles in relation to marriage discipline), the Liturgical Commission was asked to produce a slightly more authoritative text. This was issued as *Draft Services of Prayer and Dedication after Civil Marriage* (GS Misc. 193) in July 1984. Comment was to be sent to the Commission by the end of August 1984, and at its September meeting the Commission re-touched the drafts. They will be published later in 1984.

(e) BCP and Series 1 Services

The Commission has frequently discussed ways of publishing and authorizing variants on the BCP and Series 1 services, and has decided it was inadvisable to try. The action of the House of Bishops, recorded on pages 24-25 above, was a wholly independent initiative of that House.

(f) Beyond 1990

It is clear that the Commission will have a major task in the coming years to prepare for the stages in the Church of England's liturgical life which lie beyond 1990. Presumably, however, there will be a new Commission in 1986, following the election of a new Synod in 1985.

11. ECUMENICAL LITURGICAL MATTERS

Whilst the official services of the Church of England have not been expanded by ecumenical liturgical drafting in the past six years, there have been many points at which such drafting has come before the Church of England.

(a) Covenanting for Unity

The General Synod motion of July 1978 is printed out on page 4 above, and it had clear implications for the task of the Church's Council for Covenanting. The report of the 'C.C.C.' was published in Spring 1980, under the title *Towards Visible Unity: Proposals for a Covenant* (C.C.C.). A large part of the report was devoted to the liturgical proposals for the service for the inauguration of the Covenant.[1] The structure of the rite was as follows:

Ante-communion
>   Preparation
>   Ministry of the Word
>   Presentation of Documents (tabling of records and resolutions from the Covenanting Churches)— concluding with penitence
>   The Promises—interrogatory form
>   'The Act of Reconciliation'— affirmation of mutual acceptance of each other.
> [Recess]

Ordination and 'Blessing of Ministers
>   Ordination of Bishops for the various Churches
>   'Blessing' of Episcopal Ministries, uniting them
>   Ordination of Presbyters
>   'Blessing' of Presbyteral Ministries, uniting them
>   'Blessing' of Diaconal and other Ministries
>   Reaffirmation of Baptismal Promises, by all
>   Greeting of Peace
> [Recess]

Communion
>   Usual order with special Eucharistic Prayer and propers

Other liturgical material was provided in statements on baptism and confirmation, including some provision of texts for joint services, and ordination rites which followed very closely those in Series 3 (now included in the ASB).

Without touching on the Covenant's progress in the other four Churches which had been members of the C.C.C., it is sufficient to note here that it had a rough ride in the Church of England. Three anglo-catholic representatives of the Church of England on the C.C.C. dissented, giving as main reasons (though slightly opaquely at some points): the provision for not all United Reformed Church Moderators to be made bishops at the outset; the provision for mutual acceptance (by 'blessing') of presbyters (including the uncertainty as to whether this would be done exhaustively or representatively); and the provision for women presbyters to be received by the Church of England alongside the men. The General Synod in July 1980 showed hostility, and the new Synod in February 1981 sent it down

---

[1] I was a member of the liturgical sub-committee which advised on the structure and contents of the rite, and even started to speculate on whether the central event should take place in Earl's Court, or Wembley Stadium, or the Birmingham National Exhibition Centre! Car-parking and toilet facilities were important considerations . . .

to the dioceses without a two-thirds majority in each House over two of these disputed points. The diocesan returns were not notably enthusiastic, and on 7 July 1982 the Covenant reached the end of the road (Bishops 38-11, Clergy 148-91; Laity 154-71)—without a two-thirds majority in the House of Clergy, or a two-thirds majority overall.[1]

(b) Local Ecumenical Development

Following the defeat of the Covenant, the Standing Committee established a Working Party to consider 'Local Ecumenical Development', under the chairmanship of the Bishop of Derby, and this published its report in July 1984 as 'GS 642'. This defined the concept of a 'Local Ecumenical Project' and proposed ways in which the Canons governing forms of worship, and the leadership of worship, could be suspended or adapted for such defined areas. At the time of writing, it is due to be debated in the General Synod in November 1984.

(c) Ecumenical Publications

Since 1978 the Joint Liturgical Group has published: *The Daily Office Revised* (SPCK, 1978)[2]; (Ed. R. C. D. Jasper) *Getting the Liturgy Right* (SPCK, 1982); and (Ed. D. Gray) *Holy Week Services* (SPCK, 1983). The ARCIC *Final Report* (CTS/SPCK, 1982) has been debated once in General Synod, and is due to be sent down to the dioceses in 1985—and this, of course, includes eucharistic theology. The 'Lima' statement, *Baptism, Eucharist and Ministry* (WCC, 1982), was debated with ARCIC in July 1983, and is due to be sent down with it. There exists as a separate but associated document a 'Lima Liturgy' used at the Fatih and Order meeting at Lima in January 1982, and at the WCC Assembly at Vancouver in July 1983.[3] ICET has ceased to exist, but a projected 'English Language Liturgical Consultation' *(ELLC)* is due to begin meeting in August 1985.

---

[1] One tiny footnote relates to the eucharistic prayer in the inauguration rite. I objected to this (it was that in the Episcopal Church of Scotland's 1977 rite), but slightly late. The C.C.C. liturgical sub-committee redrafted, but it was not published till after the defeat of the proposals, and then it came out in *The Failure of the English Covenant* (C.C.C., 1983).

[2] This contained an 'ecumenical canon' which was one of those considered and rejected by the bishops in the early stages of creating Rite A (see Booklet 14C, p.13). It is contained in the United Reformed Church's . . . .

[3] It is published in cheap form in England in Grove Worship Series 86, *ARCIC and Lima on Baptism and Eucharist* (Grove Books, 1983).